MIRROR OF LIFE

SEASON1

LIPSITA MOHANTY

BlueRose Publishers
NewDelhi • London

© Lipsita Mohanty 2022

All rights reserved

All rights reserved by author. No part of this publication may be reproduced, stored in a retrieval system or transmitted in any form or by any means, electronic, mechanical, photocopying, recording or otherwise, without the prior permission of the author.

Although every precaution has been taken to verify the accuracy of the information contained herein, the author and publisher assume no responsibility for any errors or omissions. No liability is assumed for damages that may result from the use of information contained within.

First Published in January 2022

ISBN: 978-93-93809-39-1

BLUEROSE PUBLISHERS
www.bluerosepublishers.com
info@bluerosepublishers.com
+91 8882 898 898

Cover Design:
Abdul Razaq
(Minimalist Monk)

Typographic Design:
Namrata Saini

Distributed by: BlueRose, Amazon, Flipkart

Author's Note

This book is dedicated to my readers.

&

A small Tribute to my grandfather late Pratap Chandra Mohanty.

Acknowledgements

My thanks to my family & my loved ones, they encouraged me to be flawless. Thank you my younger sister **Priyanshi Mohanty** , she stood by me at every situation. Grateful to my teachers who believed in this step of mine & my true friends who always stay behind me to make me more stronger. Got so much motivation from my cousins so thanks for that.

Thank you so much.

Author Vishal Ved, he guided me to write & put his trust on my thought process.

Mrs. Nupur Dhingra & Mr. Abdul Razaq , they gave their valuable time to improve my skills.

Thanks a lot from the core of my heart to them who believe in me, appreciate & understand me to go ahead on this path.

Thank you the best person of my life & my inspiration **Kanchana Bala Mohanty,** my grand mother, more lucky to call her **Maa.**

Without these persons' constant encouragement I could never thought of publishing this book.

Contents

Topic 1- First priority

"*If I don't stay true to myself, I won't be able to reflect the true colours of happiness that resides therein... Love yourself and spread the happiness*"

In the present era, we always strive to look at others' perceptions and thought process, but somehow fails to survey what lies beneath us. We are too much occupied to observe others that we skip to analyse the importance of ourselves. Have you ever observed what is the "prime factor"?

Everyone is trying to pretend as the best in the eyes of others people. What they think and feel about us is of utmost priority for us, rather than concentrating on what we feel about ourselves. If someone is asking about the most prominent and precedence thing in the world, then the response would be "the present moment".

If you will question yourself about your priority, without consulting anybody, your silent eyes, the soul that resides in you, the mind that has been confused and stuffed with insignificant things, and the screaming heart would answer your question in a single sentence, i.e.

The first priority in the world is you.

Nothing is more important than you & your mind, your self-respect, your thought process, your hard work and your dreams.

If you are thinking about yourself that doesn't mean you are a selfish person. Don't forget we obtain a diamond from the cornerstones of coal. Glare yourself and then you can see the world would sparkle by your gleam. Alter your perceptions, spread the charm of happiness and then try to change the world.

Do not sit back and wait for someone else to reveal your importance to you. Recognise your worth and exhibit the hidden charisma in front of others. Never put efforts to make a false image of yourself in others' eyes. Let your aura flair your charm.

Ameliorate yourself- give priority to yourself, give wings to your ambitions and make your path. The world is a mirror and you would get what you give, likewise, if you cannot love yourself, no one would be going to love you back.

Going with the flow is not the right choice, make the flow and go with it.

"Be you".

Topic 2- Is that you?

When you wake up in the morning, walk towards the mirror and observe yourself in it for a while. Ask yourself a question, "Is that you?"

The way you have altered for others, the image transpired by your brain, and the way you have portrayed yourself in others' eyes, the way the outer world looks at you, "Is that actually true? Is that a real you?"

The possible answer you would receive is, "NO".

The truth is, in this materialistic world, the true identity of a person is hidden behind a fabricated one, which demands a person to become a splashy one. Being true to yourself would give you another positive perception of life. Don't neglect the factuality. Don't avoid your inner qualities. The world is dramatically changing into a competition, so try to expand & extend yourself, according to the requirements of the era. But do not change to make yourself visible in the eyes of others, or what they want you to become. Create your identity and let the world follow your footsteps. Don't be a part of a competition, but do competition with your yesterday. Fight to make you better than before. Try to enhance and hone your skills and become a better version of yourself. Do improvisation as much as you can and shine on your own light which is hidden in you only. Strikeout the corruption from your mind. Stay calm like the spring wind, be intrepid and be bold. Only you can explore yourself & then express your identity like the sun.

Defy every single hitch. Don't get bogged by the hurdles that come in between. They are an integral part of our life, and they would always be there once you pretend to be like some other person because you can change your identity but you cannot change the reality. Pros and cons are common in everyone's life. We can't change the reality of life, but how to Deal with that in your strong mindset, how to work on that it's totally up to you. Try to enlighten yourself and recognise your flair and then no one can snatch the path of your growth.

Listen to others, think about others' suggestions but the decision-maker should be you. Choose the right option because you are the true sorcerer of your life. You are that person who can beat every obstacle. If it's your life then why you are giving chance to you for blaming others! If something is going wrong then accept it by thinking it is just because of you only. How hard it is? You have to stand for yourself. You have to find yourself & you have to introduce yourself because nobody can understand you more than you understand yourself. You are enough for your life to live.

And once you will follow your heart and the way you are, you would observe your answer to the above-mentioned question as, "Yes, that's me!"

Eyes
express
Every
emotion
of our heart
in simplicity
better than
complication
words
from your Lips.

-Titli

Topic 3- Life is all about dreaming.

We get one life and to plan it according to our desires is not a bad thing. There is nothing wrong with dreaming big, but to fulfil them by following the right path should be your priority. If you dream big but do not indulge in the things and the means to fulfil them, then there is no meaning and would not be fair with your life too.

Noticing other's words "Dream is an imagination & it's about only forgetting". But imagination comes from your heart which you want to achieve. We dream about the things that we love to do, but that too in unconsciousness, which we are unable to understand with the glares of consciousness. So, while achieving them, one needs to wake up and work hard to achieve them. Dreams are something that compels you towards fulfilment.

The dream is not about forgetting but about fulfilling. So, see the dreams and chase them until you achieve them. Sometimes we see nightmares and that is about our inner fear. Don't feel scared after that. Fight against that fear. And if you think it's not needed then forget that without even thinking once.

Nightmares that haunt you from achieving your ambitions should not be kept along, rather bid goodbye to them and move ahead with nurturing the seed of your goals and focusing on achieving them. The first step of success is dreams. If we dream, we will understand our desires, if we understand the requirements, we will get ideas, if we get ideas, we see the path to go on. If we start walking on them, gradually we would learn to run and can achieve the desired goals. And the focus is a priority for success.

Once you would focus on your dreams and aspirations, you would find yourself close to the victory that was once dreamt by you. It would be abrupt to say here that:

"The more you conceive, the more you achieve".

Aspiration triggers hard work and dedication and it will boost your confidence to snatch the goal you want. The most essential fragment is never evacuating the ambitions you have, by the idiotic frame of references of your fellowship.

Scurry on your dreams. Shimmer it. Confer the finest from all.

See that dream which can't let you take rest from restless work towards it.

Life is a dream which is about to live with fulfilment.

Lipsita
Mohanty

Topic 4– You are beautiful just the way you are!

*W*e habitually flummox on, "Are we looking beautiful or not?"

We keep on relying on others to become judgemental about our appearance. We try to present ourselves in a way that others want to see us, their choices, their likes matter a lot to us. I don't understand, why we bestow the opportunity on others to moderate us? Aren't we sufficient to figure out we are beautiful or not?

- If your outer veneer is dark but your convection is luminous then you are "beautiful". If someone is transgender then what's a hiccup in that? If someone's outer body is burnt or has acid blitz then what's the problem? The appearance does not matter, what matters is your heart and the sense of gratitude that you have for others. There is no harm in looking different, as every human being is different from one another. Accept the gift of this beautiful life that has been gifted to you by God.

No one has the right to judge you. No matter how you look, only thing that matter is, if your intramural look is lucent... your apprehension is glossy... ideas are bright, then you are beautiful more than everything. Beauty consists of thoughts & opinions. Beauty consists of how you see others.

No one can appreciate you more, more than you admire yourself. Accept and love yourself. However, society sees you, whoever criticises you on anything, that can't decide you are beautiful or not. Admire yourself for being you and spread your charisma wherever you go. You can decide & you can prove to yourself what you are and how you are! If you can then you are beautiful "just the way you are."

Topic 5- Education

Real education is not what is being taught to us in schools or colleges, rather. It is a proficiency that how we utilise the circumstances of life and how we react towards our gloomy situations.

We don't get education only from our instructors, rather we learn it from every person around us. We should plumb our wisdom by exploring various fields. There is no specific place from where the rules of education are inculcated, we can grasp it from someone who is younger to us and someone who is having the vast experience of life. We can learn from creature and inanimate of the world.

Our knowledge should be prodigious as air. We should never assign a limit to it as there is no limit to learning. In this vast world, there is a lot to learn from every tiny creature who collects the grains by working day and night so that they can save for their tough times, and from the experienced one who had built the empires by working hard and giving everything to it.

Erase every margin on learning, opine endlessly like the sky.

Put hard effort with your maturity on the depth of your soul. It's our responsibility to pile up immense learning till our last breath.

Knowledge is everywhere if we can find it. Listening with patience is a skill. If we have that skill then we can learn. If we can learn, we can get knowledge. Learning & getting knowledge is a continuous process. Even unknowingly we learn so many things. It feels unbelievable but it's true. Knowledge can't be measurable but it can be defined by situations & experiences.

Try to hone your skills regularly, learn from everyone be it younger or older. Education is a tool to hone your charisma and it would enlighten your soul.

Topic 6– The solution to every problem is to face it.

*E*very soul on this earth has complications during its existence. Dropping your weapon in front of the troubles is not the solution to your problems. They will stand in your way until you fetch a solution to them or taste the fruit of defeat. Problems never appear to make you weaker rather they appear to make you stronger than before. Here it is not guaranteed that you would either win or lose something, rather you would either taste the fruit of success else would grab a lifetime experience to not repeat your previous mistakes.

Winning or losing is one side but get to grips with the situations containing our courage that's the holy spirit.

Ups and downs will continue and even after trying thousands of times then also we can't vanish it. So, the solution to any kind of issue is to just face it. Have patience and never lose your hope. Don't give up before the outcome will be shown. Troubles and obstacles never shatter someone, but they make someone fierce.

Topic 7- Be silent-Your success will noise one day.

The success does not see how many people have criticised you, or who all were there in your journey towards the peak, it observes your enthusiasm and dedication to achieve the desired results. People would be there to question your deeds, and they might blame you for a few things, but success occurs to those who do not get bogged by any of the hindrances and continuously move towards the achievement of their goals.

Have you ever thought, what are you doing?

And

What should you do?

The basic thing which we all know is that every action has an equal and opposite reaction. But you don't need to give any kind of explanations and answers to the question. To them who are more like a barrier between you and success.

A few of the people would be there who would backstab you during your journey, but make sure that this action should not bother you. It's common to get irritated on backstabbers, feeling alone. When everyone leaves you in the way with all your struggles, you might feel bleak and betrayed.

Think about a moment before reacting or pouring anger on such people, whether they deserved it or not? They would forget everything sooner or later, but ultimately you would end up hurting yourself which would simultaneously hamper your growth and development.

If you really want to rise then just, "Be silent".

Nowadays humans are awaiting to tow you from your grails. You should listen to them, and wait for the time when your success would speak louder. It is not mandatory to reply in words on their chirpings. Nothing can give the guarantee to stop or end the biter words of the people who denounce you other than your victory.

You have the best option to aerosol all these things, i.e.

Determination is important. Be sure about your goal which is more important than such minute things that would vanish in a blink. Pivot performance is necessary & failure is needed to inculcate you with the right choices to be made at the right moment. If you failed to achieve your desired target at once, don't get disheartened, and get up again with hope as it might be a difficult path but would certainly embellish with the gleam that would make you stand out of the crowd.

Having patience all the time is difficult but is certainly a perfect choice. Always think positive, it gives us confidence. Confidence gives us new hope and trying with hope is the key to success.

The colours of your beautiful success will surely sparkle the darkness of the difficulties. Your result will definitely clear the evil eyes of haters.

Topic 8– Sex is different, humans aren't!

We, humans, are a little selfish people on this earth. We often opined about others without looking towards the reality. We make an opinion about their deeds, appearance, actions, without even looking at the other side of the coin. One such biased opinion appears for transgenders in our society. Every community, be it of any status look at them with disesteeming eyes and does not bother about their emotions too.

In fact, 99% of people don't allow transexual people in festivals & occasions. Where a larger section of the society does not consider them equal, another section is also there that invites them to bless their families. They consider them as a blessing and give them respect whenever anything positive happens in their families.

We don't have any problem with two genders, i.e. Male & Female. But despite living in an independent country, transgenders are deprived of specific status in the community or society.

There is are many rights for transsexuals. And there is a hell & heaven gap to appreciate those rights. The veracity of the world is this world contains trio sex. Humans have faith in the deeds of God, they blindly believe in the existence of God, they make temples, mosques, gurudwaras, and churches but sometimes ignore humanity. They should accept this creation of God themselves.

It's natural to say, "God created every single cell."

Then it's our mistake to pin up them in the wrong way.

Don't make difference. They are also humans. They also have feelings. It's only us who make them feel uncomfortable. One should respect every individual despite his social status, gender, caste or appearance.

Everyone deserves to feel comfortable in the society where they are living and have the rights to work, live and fulfil their dreams and roam freely in this country. The Constitution has given them rights, and we should also change our perspective towards them.

"All deserve to be equal in our country, India, the people of God believer count on male as hero and female as angels so simply we can accept the transgender people as heroic angels.

Topic 9- Criticism affects!

Success is not available anywhere; one needs to earn it by bestowing dedication and hard work to it. People who work passionately and continuously without losing their enthusiasm due to the hindrances in their path, surely get success. Many people interfere in others' business overlooking their own things. They often comment on others for their failures or deeds, and they are the people who do not have any relation to them. They just poke in their lives because they feel it is necessary.

How stone-hearted people can pull the legs of progress-oriented humans! They are least bothered about the sentiments involved therein. They keep on interrupting their work as if that is their prime responsibility. People just say and leave. But they also pull out their negative vibes. On others that they remain within the minds of affected people, once they leave the place.

Criticizing others is very easy. And it is easier to judge others, speak badly about them, and to demotivate others.

These negative vibes impact our mental conditions and peace of mind. This negativity hampers our physical health too. Criticism is also one of the reasons why people get into depressions. It is hard to get over that. People also suffer many kinds of harmful issues. How can we avoid it if that strikes onto us? Crab nature is everywhere now. They pin us by their dominating words. We don't need to get our mind to be involved in & waste our time, and a permanent solution is in our hands that is, "Do something worthy which can't be forgettable by all". "Have faith in your instincts."

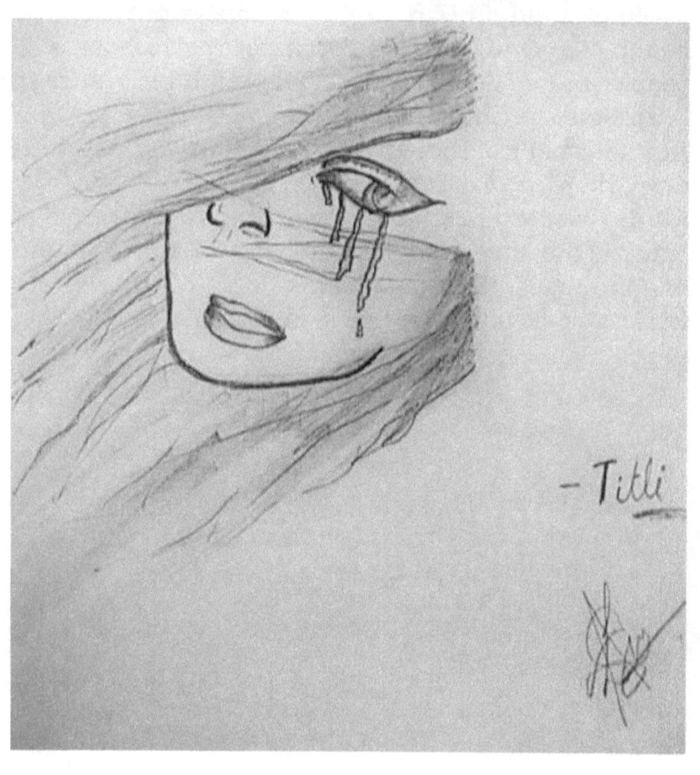

- Titli

Topic 10- Hope & expectations.

u"Where there's a will there's a way, ie. **if someone is determined to do something, he will find a way to accomplish it regardless of obstacles**." There is nothing wrong with having hope as it is a mere desire, a wish to get something, while expectations are one notch above the hope and it is a situation when one is desperate about something, which he would like to achieve at any cost. We expect something from someone & when we are expecting something and we don't get it, we reach onto a stage where we feel hurt, and betrayed. depressed feelings surmount us.

On the other hand, hope is a positive vibe and carries the ability to boost up our energy to work enthusiastically. But when the hope gets transformed into an expectation and if they are not fulfilled, we get hurt because of those anticipations.

But hope is a very positive vibe and it can boost our energy to do hard work and get that. But if we don't get that then also, we don't get hurt. Yes, we get quite upset which is very obvious because if the thing what we want is not go the same as we need then also, we feel very upset but it's ok. Because it's not a feeling of disgusted. It's simple and then also we lose hope so in every situation of life, just remember one thing that never lose hope at any cost. But also, never expect something from anyone because expectations really hurt.

Topic 11- This time will pass away.

A very common line we all listen that "Time is just like a circle" & described like once you have gone through a stage might be good or bad then definitely you will live that time again will stand at the same situation. It means whatever you do, would come back to you.

But, it's not the reality. Time is an opportunity and not a curse or blessing. The truth is, there are many unbelievable differences between listening & understanding. We react according to our situations in time.

Everyone is aware that time will run no matter what and it's never going to come again.

Then, why don't we feel that?

Sometimes a few people make us realize the value of time holding the hands of situations.

I would like to share a moment of my school life journey when I was in class 10th & that one day's one class's one line turned my lifestyle.

With my folded hands, I would like to mention the name Mr. Srinibas Panda, not only as my teacher but also considering as my father, a very kind & honest person. He randomly told in class that "This time will pass away". I did not know that line could strike in my mind but I still remember after some time, I asked him the meaning of that line & he made us understand that meaning with a very humble nature.

The meaning which is captured from him is that no matter what is happening but we should not forget that this exact time is temporary. If we are in sorrowfulness now then it's ok to cry, if we are happy now then it's ok to smile, if we are not able to understand the situation then it's ok to stick.

Because time will pass, so why get so happy that we will not even make ourselves ready to face the upcoming painful moment!

Why ~~to~~ get so much worried that we will not be able to laugh in the next joyful moment!

Just accept every situation of life. Make yourself feel & understand that this time will pass away & once it passed then it became the past. Be ready for every single challenge of life. Enjoy the happiness & also handle the bad days with positive vibes.

Time doesn't stay so don't waste a moment too, just live it.

Grateful & also luckiest to feel proud because of having a teacher who treats me as his elder daughter. Thank you so much, **Mr. Srinivasa Panda** Sir, for your valuable teachings.

Topic 12- Relationships

The relationship is not only based on the same blood. It's a bonding that is connected with feelings. And the feeling does not see any blood, cast, colours, or religion. Because it comes from the heart. It is directly connected with love, loyalty, care, trust, honest & selfless intentions.

Everyone has a name for their relationship. But everyone can't maintain that. Various types of relationships are there surrounding us but we all define every relation with a name such as father, mother, siblings, friends, life partner.... etc. But a relationship only needs saturate love to build. No matter whatever the name of relation is! Even there are also some unnamed relations that even don't need a tag name because it has love which is enough.

And belief & faith make every relation stronger day by day. Faith creates the depth of love & love creates the profoundness of connection.

Having people in our life with strong bonding who stand by us in good times and make us smile in hard times too. The relation that doesn't get apart from us in our most difficult times too then they are really rare and if we have some of them then don't leave their hand no matter how much difficult time is! Be with them for a lifetime as they can't let you cry.

The value of every positive connection is priceless & nobody can replace the love of someone for someone else in their heart. Once it is placed then it becomes our responsibility to maintain that whatever the relation is!

My first goddess **Mrs. Gayatri Mohanty**, make me understand the above these & thank you for everything.

Once a superhero told me that "whatever comes from heart, that is correct". And that person is none other than **"Mr. Bikram Mohanty"**. I am falling short in words how to thank him but still thank you because he is not only my inspiration but also my father.

Topic 13 - I

Sometimes I become a puzzle, it's hard to fix. Sometimes I become like wind, it's easy to feel.

I'm happy however I am.

I don't give rights to others to judge me. Because I know myself more than anyone else. The unstoppable time is equal to the unstoppable me. I create my own wind in which I just fly infinitely.

The girl who has no fear to be a girl & to fight against whatever the situation is, that's me.

Now I don't curse myself to be unique, to think differently, have various extraordinary dreams and I will never want to change these qualities. I accept & love myself the way I'm.

I'm the unapologetic girl who loves to make others smile, who loves to help the needy as much as she can.

Maturity comes from the situations & I clicked it in time to carry that with me forever.

Childish & a smiley girl can handle everything. But not everybody can understand me. And I don't want to be one of as I'm only the Lipsita Mohanty.

Proud & ego ruin everything.

Why should we shelter in that if we are not perfect?

The whole world is imperfect. So don't find yourself as a perfect being.

Feel yourself imperfect & work on it to be perfect till the end of the life by knowing I can never be perfect but with the understanding I can improvise myself better than before.

Yes, I am Lipsita Mohanty, the infinite girl.

On a short note, I want to share a name from which line I realized all these things about myself, a very humble, truthful, sincere and most hard-working person, one and only my top favourite sir & inspiration **Mr. Dinesh Biswal, w**ho gave me the position of his elder daughter & blessed me on teacher's day with a line **"Nothing is there which you can not do".** And this is true enough to understand me. With folded hands want to say Thank you so much for always being there with me just like my father.

www.ingramcontent.com/pod-product-compliance
Lightning Source LLC
Chambersburg PA
CBHW051504140726
47987CB00006B/2871